OFF THE GRID PRESS

L E E   S H A R K E Y

A DARKER, SWEETER STRING

Published by:

> Off the Grid Press
> P.O. Box 84
> Weld, Maine 04285
> www.offthegridpress.net

Some of the poems in this book first appeared in the following: *Green Mountains Review* ("By moonlight," "Transitory"), *The Other Side of Sorrow: Poets Speak Out about Conflict, War, and Peace* ("Eye"), *The Pinch* ("We both drink the water, neither can describe its taste," "My clothes have caught fire at both ends"), *Prairie Schooner* (the "Gift of a Cradle" sequence), *Sandy River Review* ("Intifada").

With gratitude to the Servants of the Queen Bee, who have sustained me in my writing these many years, and to Tam Lin Neville and Bert Stern for their loving but insistent editing of this manuscript.

Cover photograph by Lee Sharkey. Book design by Michael Alpert.

ISBN: 978-0-9778429-1-9 / 0-9778429-1-6

To play death on a darker, sweeter string

—Imre Kertész

CONTENTS

for Jesse, Julie, Caleb, Leo, and Al

Where the raven was

There is a stream there is milk there is a raven

There is a stream of milk there is where the raven was

There was milk there was a stream

Hoooaaa asked the raven and the raven answered *aankh*

By the stream always it is now down the alleles always it is now

Who goes there milk goes there the dead child forever leaving

The new child arriving in a pod of milk

There is sky there is a nest of sticks there is the raven drawing a circle

Overhead are branches where the raven was

Aaugh aaugh ricochets and night fish rise

In a thousand troubled throats

Who stole the milk

By moonlight we can see it spilling

In its wake the wanderers will follow

Where the raven was there was a stream the milk was stolen

The stream spills over every body floats

RETRIEVALS

Insomnia

in the house of the past
which room can we sleep in
whose breast mindlessly bury our face in

in the citrine morning
voices penetrate the walls
we were going to be happy
we were going to live like other people

firehosing the carnal debris
scrubbing the features off their faces
an old new breed grows determined

in every bedroom corpses are sleeping
in red rags of muslin

Obviously dead

soon enough the dead return and cross the threshold
Mary slouches   her belly good as gold

the salesman in the luggage of his skin
doodles maps to the exterior

the lank indifferent misplaced girls
throw down cards from time to time around the table

this is the house where no one owns her body
not a ligament but comes undone

the girls eat fate like candy
the ghost who's hungry takes advantage

       leans in   touches
       sips from their lips

Implications

residue of ink across a page
electrocardiogram of a moment struck from time

where there is no there
and a sharp incline says climb

through the subway dark

through survivors' screams

palpate the anthracite
walls are sweating

clamber soft mounds indeterminate
ground is breathing

the thick heart teems
with polyglot ravens   with coyotes upyowling

Anticipation

who then is sitting on the velvet ottoman
arm draped over what comes next

can't see the face it's not drawn yet
whose nerves will pulse a firmament of pain

someone will taste her breath ten days
in a cave in the rubble of a quake

it's enough that we live with this
without your bloody wars

mr. prime minister   don
ayatollah   image-in-chief

technosomnolent debaucher
generalissimo

Agents

who who who woke up to say I didn't
who who who woke up to say I did
who who raised naked palms before who
who cried whose face was a purple flower

who blessed the soldier fresh from killing
who who who will wear black ribbons
who wrapped grenades round whose waist like a lover
who clipped flesh and laid gauze over

who talked like a tourist while bombs arced around her
who who who flew in flew low flew over
who fired who ordered fire
who who turned away who turned away

Unwrapping silence

for Deng Feng Ping

she lives by the old teachings
she is stubborner than money

it is selling the children to the cities
dollar a day boys   dollar a day girls

riveting towers from scaffolds while we're sleeping
looming fibers we'll be shimmering in

hammering bone   rattling tendon
pitting out lungs

old man   she insisted   let your grandchild study
I'll build her a desk   find her books to carry

for two more years one child's mind stayed hungry

she is learning a language to relay her urgency

Forgotten

not one thing you made
has found a place in anyone's household
no anecdotes circulate in which you star

the perils that gathered your unnamed family
for the ocean passage go unrecorded
what your mother sang at bedtime silence shrouds

no one invokes you on the holidays
or settles down with you in mind to dream

the air bears no trace of the arc of your arm sworn to fury
no flesh remembers your withheld caress

if you had known would you have done things differently
you turning and turning in your oblivion

The suicides

we're circling the hole where the ones
who abandoned us lie   absent   electric

we're pacing a ring in the ground
to contain what they spilled

yet we can't keep our eyes off its surface
we're greedy to ladle the crimson porridge

to beat out the krik krak of tin foil and bone
then   traitors   we shout

take it back   for the sake of each morning
you summoned the figments together

for the sake of the baba whose cow fed
all the children until there was none

By moonlight

one of us will leave the other sure enough
while one of us disintegrates to never having been

one will lie beside the unsound of not breathing
eating out the night

the pact we've made is simultaneous
persistent to the brink

beyond love I've loved our animal companionship
our spooning as we wake and sleep

whoever holds the dying other
will inhale one last time in unison

both of us will listen
to the green incessant wind

Transitory

we were an industrious species
our lights strung the planet with hampers and nests

in thin steel pods we filed
across expanses we drained and fertilized

to grow our rows to feed our appetite
for hatch and crosshatch

to speculate the atom
we built an engine blue as fire

it swarmed the seven continents
it oversaw the clouds to the round horizon

its moving finger weighed   divided
scripting the news of our dominion

UNSCRIPTED

Unscripted

First word first
the lustral word
the word for mother

When desire has fled   what holds the center
holding the center
only one desire

This sack of skin
his eyes   ever a window

in sleep   transparent lids

his eyes
there is no time

breathe in   breathe out

pain in the center
inside the sack   a cavity

sun has never touched

I grew a child
and in that sack   a cavity

a dark accord

at the base of the skull
a tangled flow
a flower

§

It was not the strangling of a fabled city
900 days   900 nights

    it was a hard thing   following a hard thing
    in rooms of anxious strangers pain had gentled

it was not tent city   cold mud sliding
through the shoes of displaced bundled hundreds

    it was antiseptic
    fear and hope were hothouse flowers

it was not cluster bombs   snipers' fire   shrapnel
it wore no M-16   did not click its heels

    it held its breath
    counting to forever

it was not a nation   grieving
a generation of its young

it was rending
keening

there were no villains   nor was it a plot
no goon squads   black marias   machete swinging priests
there was no wall of skulls

wind blew cold
the blade cut cleanly through the skull
it was my child

§

A woman in pain am I
a folding skeleton with ribs for wings

my precious   my golden   my mortal   my own

spirit of my son   don't slide away
spirit of my child   stay with him

in my chest is a hollow
a bird with folded wings

this is the road I'm on
this is the space I'm in

      no world beyond
      his face   his breathing

      floating in a sack of time
      no mother womb

this is the street we're on
this is the road we're walking

      Blessed art thou
      suspirer of the universe
      wingbreaker
      healer of wings

      §

The parts were   *mother*   *child*
My lines   *I've seen him through*
made good on all my vows
to stay alive until he'd grown

The script read
Now he's mated   *moved*   *settled*
strong   *supple*   *skilled*
my bounding boy come true

The script promised
You won't see him suffer
you won't see him die—
he'll *lose* you

The script said
This is ground   you walk
when you lie down
it supports you

§

The morning
              I walked to the marsh
holding my child's hand in my left hand
              Death in my right
there at the tip
              of the sentinel tree

you were   sudden   pure   white
tall   wide shouldered black   masked
real   apparition

you looped
              overhead
spread wings
              deepening air
and made it
              the only element
that agora of song
              your wings were carving

§

When pain racked him
  when his whole body spasmed
when the kneading of these hands that knew him
  for their own no longer gave him respite
when night lengthened
  when he could not sleep and thrashed exhausted

he said *Stay with me*

I crawled into his bed
  stretched my length alongside his
  pressed my chest against his back
held his chest
  eased my breath

   so he could sleep

  once again

by my heartbeat

§

Suppose we could see them
the lines traced by creatures
            the heat of their night cries

                    tracing infinity
        one of its loops
                    drawn to a long   arced   circling

                    §

                    Pluck the marble
                    fingertip and thumb
                    this is how the brain relearns to speak

up stairs
down stairs
left hand   right foot
right hand   left foot

                            consciousness traveling the spine

        under the drifting surface
        under the puckering
        quick
        water lilies have weathered the winter

have risen from mud
for the surface
where new leaves lie
green and exposed

a child
came on water gold blooming
stems drawn
from an unfathomable bottom

stroke   feather
guiding the paddle
pulling it down
through the deep

learn as the child does
proximal to distal
finger play last

sky paints water
monochrome clouds
sculpt bone hollows

traveling the spine

lilies are steeping
sky is incised
with speaking

dredged
from the unspeakable

call   response from a distance
tug in between

remembering   reminding
to speak

who can speak this yellow
source of the pouring
over the water
into the shimmer

where hawks sweep
wingtip to wingtip
scanning a whorl
of desire and devouring

arms held wide
in a line with the shoulders

wingfeathers   spread

listen

lilies have risen
from mud   for the surface
where new leaves lie
shining   exposed

        cups
                open
        red lines the throat

                at the base of the skull
      a tangled flow
                a flower

EYES

Intimate horizon

for Bianca, for Emily

Another sixty years you may have of
crossing the breadth of this planet picking
up and discarding stones from your pockets
on the wooded path leading to the slope
of the avalanche fearful and amazed
as I have been these sixty years your hearts
lighting with desire when I have long since
laid down my heat to compost   What you see
from the mountain I will not not the flood
nor the plague nor the long dry wasting nor
will I hear your footsteps when you arrive
once more with a gift to feed a migrant
band   one of the many small beginnings

In vigil (2)

If the whole body is a heart, then the woman who steps out of the
car with Texas plates to yell at the silent peace vigil is a heart
overlaid with hate

*I have two children in the war and let me tell you: They are the
heroes, you don't deserve to walk this earth*

A mouth pursed over pain

*I'll take the opportunity to tell you about my family. My son's no
"stupid soldier"—got a master's degree. He went to Iraq to bring
democracy*

Slides into her car's steel shell and slams the door. Glass can't hide
what's writhing up her, what compels her to climb out and tell

Now he lives from minute to minute. . . .

*Do any of you know what it's like to be up all night, every minute
thinking*

School photo of a dark-haired girl, blurred under plastic. She
shows it, half grandmother-proud, half defiant. *She's seven and
misses her daddy. A little girl needs her daddy*

No! jumps back, *I don't care what you have to say*

But I am forming words for her. I want to touch her cheek and say them

I recall the waiting room, the surgeon's teeth, the monitor, months of terror, my own son's heart set totally on his pain

I would wrap my arm around her, pull her close, say quietly, *I see what it would cost to see your country has betrayed you*

Intifada

Wind this story
tight around an
olive so the
letters pierce it
and absorb its
oil

There where fingerprints
meet fruit how many whorled
signatures have sealed a
history that insists
now through leathern silvered
leaves

The pickers hear it while
they fill slung pouches and
tilt their chins to let it
brush their cheeks the ones who
planted trees have never
left

Two thousand years they've tapped
high branches swinging long
sticks ripeness has fallen
to nets children's children
lift together from the
ground

They call this home they call
this day's work expressing
oil from plump black golden
sustenance to pour
and pass from hand to hand
though

When bulldozers
brazenly up-
root this story
deafened children
lurch into the
wall

Eye

A rubber-coated metal bullet struck Ziad's eye during clashes in Bethlehem. . . . His eyeball fell in the palm of his hand and . . . he kept holding it till he reached the hospital. He thought they could put it back in.
　　　　　　　　　　　—Muna Hamzeh, *Refugees in Our Own Land*

What do you do with an eye in the cup of your hand?

What do you see that you didn't?

What do you make of a sphere of jelly with fins of torn muscle?

What do your fingers impress on the rind?

Do you rush it to hospital, where a surgeon waits to fuse sight
to vision?

Does the eye have a nationality? a history?

Does the eye have a user name?

Its own rubber bullet?

Where is the eye transcribed?

A little globe there and you are the keeper

Of the watery anteroom, the drink of clear glass

Dear eye

Once it lay snug in fat in its orbit

Once it saw as a child

Through humor a peppering of stars

Shroud

for Ruwan Abu Zaid

Some dazed heart pulled the trigger   stole the breath
some gorged heart failed to remember

how it feels to be three and released
from night's forever shapeless terror
when your grown brother after looking
down and up the now-quiet street smiles says
Yes and your legs not containable
no you do not want your sister's hand
you want open air ballooning you
to run as far as you can see the
candy store reach in the jar for a
taste of sweet to right the world by bliss

Petition

1. The heart is a pansy. The hole blown through it is its face

2. When their homes were exploded they lay down to sleep in a leaf

3. Water pours from a cleft in graffiti'd rock

4. If you look into his eyes you will be petrified

5. I am two women, each of us exhausted

6. Tears blur the foreground, smoke blurs the background, the small green plant is in focus

7. Copter fire across the circuits

8. Come from another place to die here

9. God's food, she called it, that gelatinous omelet

10. Ribcage of fire surrounding two burnt groves

11. No one there in the eyes to say, "J'accuse"

12. Framed by my hair my forehead flushes

13. Framed by the veil my cheeks are swollen

14. I looked into his eyes and became death's junkie

15. A burn hole shaped like a country

16. As if we were twins, one in a wild print, one in a chador

17. As if we were leopards devouring an impala

18. My family hid in a leaf, not moving

19. I have seen this

20. The hole in the fire, persistent

21. The haunting, fraught and persistent

22. God, we have done with your cooking

23. Having died, I am waiting for nothing

World without end

There came the time we were moved to move into the rubble

For myself, it was the only anodyne for madness. But we all had our reasons—worms in the fruit, a fine-grained poison that sifted from the ceiling, a child's accusation, snakes in the walls that hissed, *Your nest is next*

We packed nothing but a bottle of water and a rag to wipe the sweat, then crossed our thresholds, leaving the doors wide open, leaving the books to mice and the wind

Sunlight dazzled in the rising dust. The rubble made a new horizon, an angular assemblage across our line of sight

Concentrating, we picked our way over the concrete, steel, and glass that had been our expression

When we came upon living beings, they neither welcomed nor dismissed us. We ferried water and we ferried stone. What rose from their dark throats we will not mention

When the rockets and planes stopped flying, fighters and pilots took their places among us. Each sat alone looking out on his handiwork. The world grew perfectly still

We know nothing of the future; the present is true to itself. If someone groans, we do our best to give comfort. There is no hope to offer and we offer none

Snow so silent

Snow all white but for one bent stalk

One bent nail of a bird call as much sense as the day will offer

One suede pouch for the names of the fallen. Ar ra lan do pan du ra My la Mar a vi llo sa. The syllables mumble in the dark

One voice augers its way through the churning, saying *Dear dear clear*, saying *Heart*

So many of us, many of us one by one

And then again an ample table set for all plus one

In the company of grace, Per a lez Ka ro laz Ca si ka Ja ko niuk Pos pi sil I da nan Pe ar row Ka rim Re al li Is ma il San tos

Each one buries all the dead

Dud kie wicz Clay Ikh las

Awake

Well, he said, *I can't read much anymore*

Every word leaves memory's fingerprints on skin

Still, I read until I cannot sleep

MIGRATIONS

Terrain

A morning

Palm print against layers of mist

There has been some kind of mistake

Departure is impossible until further notice

The ground ticking with spores. Rust red smells like tobacco

They give me a permit that was good for yesterday

Three hundred million years and counting, long arms waving,
delicate, dusted, etched, hypnotic, undulating

Polymorphic, broken, haunted . . . with no possibility of restoration

Baby-faced soldiers barking illogical orders

A cruel man is like a razor blade. The cut surprises and the flesh
remembers

*In the end, the growers fed flowers to herds of goats and sold the
rest for a shekel a bunch on every street corner*

Forgetting takes a thousand years

No end of irreconcilable accounts

§

A night blooming tropical plant whose fragrance sickens

In bed curled like a fern as branches snap below

We do not see our way clear to respond to you in detail

Abasement is never enough. The blue silk shame seed bursts from its pod

Pales of settlement, hermetic closures

If only we could read the planets, if only we could get a little higher

Coughing and flapping their hands to ward off heat and claustrophobia

Let us set off in the moonlit woods to lose ourselves

Hay-scented, bracken, ostrich, cinnamon, squirrel foot, silvery glade

Don't think that you're really seeing us

To find ourselves at the center of the universe, in every direction a story of earth's heave and fall

The burden of homelands

You may not like this. You may slam the door. Others have done
the same

Still, it whispers to you, breaks you out in sweat when you attempt
to sleep. It whispers loud as gold your incoherence

It palpates the body, which longs for it like heart for razor wire.
But bodies are not enough

Enter the grounds of The Castle, ID card at hand. You may be
stopped at any moment. Prepare your excuses

You have forfeited the right to come here. You cannot claim the
right to go. You may be here on Monday but not on Monday night

You may go there to plant; your children may not. You may go
there to plant but not to harvest. The fruit falls down

So. Pace the stone maze even wind cannot escape

Escape, then, to the sunsets of your childhood. There you sit,
gazing at the terraced hills, the stones your sheep, tree roots
drinking from your palm

Here, you thirst but you can't drink. The river flows by you on its way to Euphoria. The power flows by you on its way to Castle Keep

So. Slip on your shades. Say good morning with the accent of the oppressor. Simulate the gender the oppressor speaks

Or. You can go by tunnel. Maybe you can get to the hospital before we bleed to death. The baby is a time bomb

The boy soldier weeps behind his shield. The girl soldier films you

They build a wall around it. They call it their familiar. It tells them, you have to choose between your mother and your father

The kids throw stones. Now. Organize your anger and set out over the disfigured landscape

Separation wall

She is leaping down from an unfinished section of it. Not who you would expect—a grown woman in headscarf, slacks, and a black ankle-length coat. In her hand are a purse and a book with papers tucked in it. Aah, she is going to school

What does the green plastic liter soft drink bottle her sturdily shod feet are about to land on study all day at the wall's feet? Wall as in *worship,* as in *worse*

I will lay me down in peace and sleep, for only thou, Lord, maketh me to dwell in safety

After the '48 war, in the Negev, all the Arabs in X who had not fled were herded inside one building and held there a month. Day, night, day, night, day, night, day, night, day, night, day night night night. The conquerors called it *The Ghetto*

In L'vov, the Einsatzgruppe lined Jews up against the wall of the sports school and shot them. Fifty years later, I searched for the holes, touched the green grass, searched for anyone who remembered

Snake, strangling intestine, sight after blinding, shiver of concrete, pre-stressed for profit, erectile dysfunction

On the highway, painted with landscapes verdant in arches

We went to bed at the usual hour. By the time we awoke, a wall had sprung up in our village. My cousin can't get to his goats. I can't get to my cousin's

They are riding a horse and a donkey alongside the wall. They are smiling. The creatures have nothing to say; they bend at the knee and move forward. *Fuck,* says the wall, awaiting its mural

In the village of Q a girl whose new front teeth are just cutting through has discovered a plaything. Delighted, she kneels on top of a slab and looks down on temptation

The farmer, the wall, the olives. The oil is bursting their skins

In the village of B you can't get to the olive groves for the concertina wire and soldiers. Shining barbed circles a foot could get stuck in. Incisored. A gaggle of women is singing the wall to oblivion. Soldiers mute as a wall hold shields for protection. Someone please kiss them then lead them away

What goes through her head in this split second between *leap* and *land*? Once again she's escaped weight, her gold scarf flying

Parable of the peach

The peach was perfect, vulva-clefted, never been refrigerated, fragrant in blush

She had been saving it for breakfast, imagining the burst when she bit in

A company of soldiers, breakfasted on rations, helmeted and shielded, gusseted with canisters and rifle-slung, arrived by dark

Ringing the village. The unassailable perfection of the ring

Sunrise brushed the dust and turned sleep inside out

Their noose of words: *Curfew, closed zone*

She'd been about to bite

Pots, water tanks clanged outrage from the rooftops

The peach in her hand, hot, soft . . .

Flung through the air at a boy soldier

She, radiant. He, as if his mother had slapped him

A piano before the wall

Here where sound grenades are the local music

According to the Code of Purity in Arms

What power might ten arched fingers playing Schubert have to
dissuade

Over sinuous roads the piano traveled, upright and dusty, untuning,
a wonder that it should come at all

The bearded traveler follows

In the white sack of memory a small boy lies curled. His mother
hands him to a stranger, her face a caul. His is a knife blade

The pearls of war within him, swallowed whole and saved

And children gather

O muse, insinuate through angry silt

In the arsenal of resistance: slingshots, peaches, balloons filled with
chicken shit, ears stuffed with cotton, printouts of "The Scream"

A piano on a truck bed in an olive grove beside a bulldozer

Melody a thin thread, bioglue, a lamplight under the flesh

We both drink the water; neither can describe its taste

From a deep well, pumped through polyvinyl and copper pipe, then out a faucet

Disrobing, you draw a bath, soap every round and crevice, lean back, cleared of forethought

From an earthwork catchment a half day's walk from the aqal. Fill two bladders stitched of skins, pack them on the camel

After sex, the ritual cleansing—the dipper, the shallow bowl. Left hand wets a cloth and runs it over the rip in the stitched vagina

Gift of light, finger of wind and palm of gravity. In the song about water you are singing a song about water

The last infrastructure frontier for private investors

In the convoy escaping the city fifteen women came into labor at once. There was no water for the midwife to wash her hands. There was no water to wet the women's lips. What can assuage the terrible thirst of the women? They left the ground beneath the galool tree covered with membrane and placenta

Discontinuities are likely. We will be well positioned to profit even more significantly when they occur

In the camp, there was no water to wash our clothes. The bandits entered. The shame of semen is ever in my nostrils

Water carried the house downstream. The flood was steel brown and thunderous. No one could stay away. It was like seeing blood coursing through the arteries of God

Sliding down the throat, cooling the tube of the esophagus. A small wave arriving in the stomach's pool

My clothes have caught fire at both ends

Licking the tempered glass face of the woodstove

Instrumental in branding, as with the tip of a cigarette held to the thigh

Blinking, Lucifer's small eyes, over the marsh

Gold in the sun! he chuckled, collecting their jewelry in a greasy cap. She risked keeping hers in her knapsack. The next stop was windowless, barbed wired. The gold disappeared while she slept

The girl lay in a fever. Her mother wrapped her in cool wet sheets

A short flash dialogue ensues between male and female

Take off your clothes. Or, not a word spoken. Contempt so intense it delivers the burn on the inside

Desire so intense that she eats him, mandibles cracking his skull

Turns out she'd stolen the jewelry to spare her daughter. Turns out they didn't

Sometimes they signal in unison, turning the marsh on and off. Which raises the question, for whom

How many men have I killed for the sake of those beasts with the excellent udders?

I watched my house burn, learned I too was combustible. Thin-skinned small planet with fire at the core

Fire's fool, womb ripper, glad-hand destroyer. Boy. *Father, I've stolen your fire*

From the place where the house was, scorched paper blew in an updraft. *Man in the fire. Afire!*

Earth come of lullaby of earth

Covered in ferns, the fertile sori dark against fronds

Punctuated by sisal and acacia. Long roots spread horizontal veins
across the surface

Owned, unownable and whose to know

Young man, who are you shooting at?

The figure that moves across it, stipe and blade brushing her shins

Teeming with micropresence

Me? for there is no enemy in sight

Though *Eloquence*, you say, *is a vice in women*, I am no camel and I
will speak

We labor to bring forth

Dig out the long, fist-thick galool root and plant both ends, the
perfect arc between

This is the vault of her vessel

Home's body, rubbing wool to flesh

Earth supplies everything that goes into it

Ribs of galool, sisal stripped, dried, pounded, shining women-
woven mats longer than bridal trains the house's skin

Skins are her trousseau. A woman is valued by the smoothness of
her skins

The house a body, portable, a turtle shell and all that seethes within

Birth fluids should be spilled where blood has spilled, you say,
trading our girls as wives

Though the breast that contains milk cannot, you say, *contain
intelligence*, my lullaby will tell the truth

I have tasted the comfort of home again. Don't drive me off on
fear's caravan

The vulture has already circled my bones and the bones of my
children, tucking its wings

White for anger, white for sorrow. We tied white bands around our
heads

In the air, spell where a drum

Habitat of exhalation

Demesne for parabolic dip and swing. Slipping pinfeathers through the shock waves

A wall of wailing holds the warriors at bay. It rises from women's throats

The covenant of speech was sealed here

Razorblades, bayonets, daggers. Not a sound was coming from my mouth

In the wing whistle of the primaries, a lure, a warning

In my hut, before my children

Trumpet creeper, jewelweed, thistle. The sword bill slips into the flower

When he learned, my husband took my ration card and threw me from the compound. I am treated like a prostitute. I want to be buried alive

1200 heart beats per minute feeding. 50 mph escaping

Burn frankincense to stir the djinn. *Tar* and *tabla* draw pain from the throat

It bites the belly and it shames them, it bites the nipples off, it shames them, it slices red ribbon and it shames them

Stuck their needle beaks right through her headcloth into her hair and beat their wings

Tossing the head and swaying, tossing the head and swaying

Zar, za zum, zar zar za zum

Aaah, now they have netted it in rhythm

A nest of down held with spider silk

The words let down

Wound flies out over the Gulf of Aden

Over the gulf, the great migration

Legend has it in the breast feathers of a swan

Washed, wrapped in new cloth, led to my threshold

Return to the self-same yard

You live here. I live here

Living as a wild thing

It is here, in the Republic of the Imagination, that we are most humane.
—Azar Nafisi, "The Stuff that Dreams Are Made Of"

Listening to Brahms, riding out on the strings, I realize that war has become the landscape of my imagination and ask, what if I withdraw that recognition

In the name of the raven—*(c)rraugh*—who occupies the sky

In the name of those who have passed into the thickness of thought, that we wear like a hood and mantle

In the name of the pine duff and the green stars that feed on our remains

It's raining in Teheran. Crackety crack go the drops on the skylights. A student is lying in bed listening to rain's language, thinking how, like a lover, it disinters the mind

In Teheran, when people *wish to empty their hearts* they turn to poetry

And swallows will lay eggs / in the hollows of my ink-stained hands

Come, come, whoever you are. / Wonderer, worshipper, lover of leaving

In love with a wild thing. In love with a face and the secrets it covers

A student plays Brahms through the crescendo/decrescendo of sirens

A bow waves like an épée over the belly of a cello

All winter, snow falls on Teheran, whitening the grey city, lightening the student's steps

The violin bow is a strand of mercury drawn down ever so slowly until the last of it rests on the string. I hold my breath while the aftertone condenses to a silver bead

Sufficient to the day

Muscles, filaments, brushstrokes, glistening organs

A song sufficient to the day, to the body in the world

The ocean has the viscosity of heavy oil, all that weight in its basin. It heaves and falls under the moon's broad tread. The gunmetal sheen of its footprint

They took the pulse of her tumor, then closed her up again

There is a degree of sleeplessness, of rumination, of the historical sense, which is ultimately fatal to the living being, whether this be a person or a people or a culture

We can see nothing beyond the tiny boat we're depending on to ferry us—oh, maybe a line of smoke, the hump of an island, a ghost destroyer at 3 o'clock, its cargo of crumpled sailors

The one who cannot sink on the threshold of the moment and forget the past

Spent all night hammering a sea of coffins

who cannot stand balanced like a goddess of victory without growing dizzy and afraid

The children are seasick. We stroke their hair, plant kisses on their foreheads, feign surety to reassure them

will never know what happiness is—

We arrive where the ghost of beauty whispers through the sand, shaking out crystals, tracing arteries and ferns

Let her die in the arms of her family

A boy tracks sea glass

In a net of voices she has never not known

Where tide paints sand with a thick impasto

worse, he will never do anything to make others happy

How beautiful is the gift of mourning

Keep swimming, we call out, the ocean knows no rest

GIFTS

Dumky

The one who has been silent is the one who sends a message to the
future

The thought that surfaces, the foreboding detail washed against
the shore

How I might sleep, were I surrounded by my father's intention to
love me

Lifetimes gathered in the body of the cello. You bow them into
memory's cradle

Oh, my love, you bare your passion in your sostenuto

But fear! Too easy to come by: the father terror becomes the terror
of the flood

What did forgetting teach but forgetting? What did withholding
teach but to withhold?

Each breath was a heartbreak. Each touch, more than a body
could bear

The underthrum, the handing off from one voice to another

Gifts

I

The nib of the pen in his mind writes a poem each night he is
imprisoned

Each night he recites all the poems he has written

On the thousandth night he writes no poem but recites 999

In exile, he draws down the shade and begins transcribing

Remembering, he lets up the shade to a land of strangers

I will never forget the press of his hands on my ribcage

2

He carries the sear in his chest to the ocean bottom

So he can bear the weight of the death of the future

Fish eat his once-ravenous eyes

He abandons himself to their kisses

Only then, only then when he is nothing can it begin:

Speaking through bones, his tears washing our cheeks

3

All he says is

In the atomic ruins

one tree

came into bud

Nine times slowly he repeats this

His is the kindest voice

4

At night I imagine the long wait of the prisoner, pride of his father, the scholarly boy

Memory's black-backed mirror reflects the heat of his longing

The father stares down darkness, letters not received

Before the prisoner, words are nothing

The hours ride by on the backs of the abducted

Slip through with me to what might have been

Lovely

beneath the lovely curve
of the horizon rests a baby

the *om* of lovely
nests in a mother's breast

the sweet stream slips
in a sinuous meander

the curved air plays
a celebratory cello

a wet mouth
is shaping vowels

On the anniversary of the invasion

on my side   knees bent   hand resting
lightly on my rib cage

lightly   your knees touch my knees
your breath washes over my face

my breath washes over your face
our breath sifts out the window

and rides the thermals
over earth's face scarred and shining

brushing distant faces
turned slightly to the touch of wind

Gift of a story

two old women dug a pond
to make a home for piggybacking frogs

a cow came to drink there
what profits one belongs to all

in bounded the neighbor's hound
then shook the good news all over

children arrived with spoons and pail
to dig up worms and cast their lines

by moonlight lovers stole there
bobbed for apples on the waves

Curve

with one hand he grabs the baby's feet
and hoists the legs so with the other
he can wash the baby bottom

his hands and the baby's limbs
have refined the configurations

by which he knows the baby
by which the baby knows him

as in another time his mother
held his feet and *upsadaisy*

we is a curve being born

Neither mother nor lover

today the war dead failed to make the headlines
to keep myself human I construct a shrine of words

a layer of tissue   a layer of salt
a little teepee with names hometowns and ages

images grafted from broadcast burials
I caption fold and tuck inside

a moment in stillness for absence
for the grief that scours the heart

a spill of thread   a spill of sand
a white stone for persistence

Cradle

they're gangly   grown   but this night
the last poem folded   the farewells said

rather than wake them
we bend and heft one more time
more weight than we can carry

as we step out into the night and stand
in knee-high grasses
they stir and settle on our shoulders

the moon slides past the Balm of Gilead's lament
in the bristling silence of the galaxy

Look again

At first I took it for a vulture
that gliding inscribed circumference,
sentinel of the dead

Next I knew it for a raven
keeling through diffuse brightness,
and I inconsequent beneath

It flew straight off, became
a muscled wavering into vapor
while everywhere the watchfulness continued

Post-war deployment

It is thought that cows' unhurried lowing,
the rise and fall in the evening of toad ululation,
the dense sweet penetration of grasses
in air drawn through the nostrils and deep into lungs
will offer our minds a place to return to
from the caves where they cower,
that the route back may be read
in the riffling surface of streams
below which bones are caressed by cold current

It is thought with the sight of the pain bird alighting
and preening each of its feathers gold and particular
that silence will hang like a peach
until one of us reaches to pluck it
and keening begins that will last through exhaustion,
that does not punish or lie

PETITION
Each image corresponds to a visual image in an on-line petition "signed" by
Israeli artists in protest against the 2006 Lebanon War. See Maarav: Drafted Art,
http://maarav.org.il/draftedart/.

TERRAIN
"Polymorphic, broken, haunted. . . ." —from Carolyn Forché, notes to *The Angel
of History*.
All other words in italics are from Amira Hass, *Drinking the Sea at Gaza*.

THE BURDEN OF HOMELANDS
The title is borrowed from Edith Noel's "Desierto."

PARABLE OF THE PEACH
A PIANO BEFORE THE WALL
The construction of a "separation barrier" between the residents of the
Palestinian town of Bil'in and their farmland has provoked non-violent protests,
weekly improvisations in which imagination, at least symbolically, triumphs over
force.
"The pearls of war within him. . . ." —Ibn Khaldun via Brian Turner's "Dreams
from the Malaria Pills (Barefoot)."

WE BOTH DRINK THE WATER; NEITHER CAN DESCRIBE ITS TASTE
EARTH COME OF LULLABY OF EARTH
The title of the first poem was prompted by Susan Mitchell, in *The Poet's Note-
book*.
Much of the content of these poems has been adapted from *Somalia: The Untold
Story*, ed. Judith Gardner and Judy El Bushra.

MY CLOTHES HAVE CAUGHT FIRE AT BOTH ENDS
"How many men have I killed. . . ." —adapted from Faarax Afcad, "Camel
Rustling," in *An Anthology of Somali Poetry*, trans. B. W. Andrzejewski.
One thread in the poem is drawn from Slavenka Drakulić's *S.: A Novel about the
Balkans*.

IN THE AIR, SPELL WHERE A DRUM
Somali women in refugee camps have been using the *zar* cleansing ritual to help
victims of rape reintegrate themselves psychologically and reclaim their place
within their social networks.

LIVING AS A WILD THING

"wish to empty their hearts" —Abbas Kiarostami, in *My Sister, Guard Your Veil; My Brother, Guard Your Eyes: Uncensored Iranian Voices*, ed. Lila Azam Zanganeh.

"And swallows will lay eggs. . . ." —Forugh Farrokhzad, "Another Birth," in *Another Birth: Selected Poems*, trans. Ismali Salami Zanbankadeh.

"Come, come, whoever you are. . . ." —Rumi, in *Look! This is Love: Poems of Rumi*, trans. Annemarie Schimmel.

SUFFICIENT TO THE DAY

"There is a degree of sleeplessness, of rumination. . . ." —Nietzche, "Untimely Meditations."

DUMKY

Dvořák's piano trio Opus 90 in E minor is commonly referred to as the "Dumky," a Czech word that suggests fleeting thoughts.

GIFTS

This poem comes of hearing testimony by Nguyen Chi Thien, Majid Naficy, and Yasuhiko Shigemoto at The Resilience of the Human Spirit: An International Gathering of Poets at the Guthrie Center in Stockbridge, Massachusetts, in September, 2006.

In 1974, Lee Sharkey bought a hundred-year-old Pearl platen press, taught herself to set type and print, and produced over the course of a long Maine winter her first poetry chapbook. Over the next four years, under the imprint South Solon Press, she printed two more chapbooks of her own poetry, portfolios of other poets' work, and ephemera such as poems on paper lunch bags.

Since then, she has continued to work both on and off the grid as a writer and an editor. Her publications include two other full-length volumes, *Farmwife* (Puckerbrush Press, 1977) and *To A Vanished World* (Puckerbrush, 1995), a poem sequence in response to Roman Vishniac's photographs of Eastern European Jewry in the years just preceding the Nazi Holocaust. In 1997 she received *Zone 3*'s Rainmaker Award in Poetry, judged by Carolyn Forché. Recent poems have appeared in *Green Mountains Review, Margie, Nimrod, The Pinch,* and *Prairie Schooner.* Since 2003 she has co-edited the *Beloit Poetry Journal,* one of the country's oldest and most respected poetry journals.

She lives in the woods outside of Farmington, Maine, with her husband, Al Bersbach, and stands in the weekly Women in Black peace vigil in front of the Farmington post office.